Growing Up With War
in the Netherlands
by
Anne M. J. Smiddy

ISBN: 978-0-9965628-1-2

Copyright © 2016 by Anne Smiddy. All rights reserved.

No part of this publication may be reproduced, stored in a Retrieval system or transmitted in any form or by any means, electronic, mechanical, photocopying, recording, scanning or otherwise, except as permitted under Section 107 or 108 of the 1976 United States Copyright Act, without the prior written permission of the author.

Printed by
The Lexington Press, Inc., Lexington, Massachusetts   U.S.A.

Printed in the United States of America.

Foreword

This booklet is written to tell you what World War II was like for a teenager growing up in the Netherlands. It describes in detail how the battle of Arnhem (1944) was experienced.

For more information on the battle I recommend the book "Arnhem 1944 the Airborne Battle" by Martin Middlebrook (Penguin Books USA Inc. 375 Hudson Street, New York, New York 10014 U.S.A.)

After the battle I kept a diary until the end of the war.

My dream was that there would never be a war again. In the late 1950s I started writing my memoirs, joined a group of Veterans in Lexington, Massachusetts, U.S.A., gave a few lectures in different places for friends. Recently I decided to publish my book.

All proceeds from the sale of this book will be donated to the International Rescue Committee, 122 East 42nd Street, New York, NY 10168.

Acknowledgements

For many years I have lived with these World War II stories close to my heart and I am thankful for all my friends, especially at Brookhaven who encouraged me to write this book. Winifred Skolnikoff's judgment was so very important to me. She gave me confidence to carry on. Further I want to mention Hannah Chandler, Thorne Griscom and Mary Ertman helping me with my English grammar and Margot Lindsay for the final proofreading. Thank you all. Without you and Bob Sacco, the publisher, I would never have accomplished what I set out to do.

From the archives of the town of Ede Vincent Lagerwy wrote an account of the documents of the time, 1940 –1945 and the counselors of the town decided to publish it in 1989. The publisher was Gert Plekkringa BDU BV Barneveld. The story of Jacob, head of the Civilian Protection Agency and his 18 year old secretary came from this book.

My son, Gerard Smiddy has created an email address (amjsmiddy@hotmail.com) to receive comments and questions about this book.

On page 5, *History of Castle Doorwerth* was taken from *Van een groene zoom aan een vaal kleed* by E. J. Demoed, published by C. V. Adremo, Oosterbeek, Netherlands 1953.

My Home in Doorwerth

My Home in Doorwerth

Above my bed hangs a picture of the house in which I was born. It is a black and white photograph taken by my father in the summer of 1929. Father, Wilhelmus Jacobus van Zanten Jut, had the house built by architect Kees Westra, before he married my mother, Catharina Maria Bloemendaal, in September 1928. My father was 38 years old and my mother 21.

The photo shows a comfortable medium to large house with white brick walls reaching to the second level. Above is a dark brown stained wood paneling, all covered with a thatch roof. Built out from the house is a bow windowed room with glass doors in the center leading to the terrace. The balcony on top is edged with planters full of red geraniums and blue lobelias. The house is surrounded by lawns, shrubbery, trees and flower beds. Father's car is parked on the white graveled driveway. At the bottom corner of the photo is a baby carriage in the shade of some trees. Although you cannot see me, I am in the carriage, completing the idyllic picture.

Father must have been a very happy man. All his dreams were coming true: a beautiful house and garden, a lovely wife and his first child. I, Anne Marie Jose, was born on the 15th of June, 1929. Every time I look at this photo I am moved by the good memories. For me it presents beauty, love and care I received. It shows quiet peace, prosperity and stability. However, shortly after I was born the stock market fell. This must have affected my father's finances severely although he never spoke about his financial affairs. He was a caring father, always making sure that we had the very best of everything.

When I was seven or eight years old he became seriously ill, probably with coronary heart disease. From then on he could not smoke his cigars and cigarettes. He became short tempered and I was afraid of him.

Hanneke, my sister, was born two years after me. She was a sharp witted child and very active, amusing the family.

The most important person in my life was my mother. Without her I would never have become the woman I am now.

Mother -1945   Mother and I - 1930

Mother knew at sixteen that she was going to marry my father. Of course her father, Gerard Willem Bloemendaal, thought she was far too young for that. He sent her to a ladies' college at Cheltenham in England, where she learned to speak English fluently and behave like a lady. They had very strict disciplinary rules that Hanneke and I learned from her.

Mother and I had an exceptionally close relationship that started right from my birth. The nurse had washed and dressed me and was on the point of putting me in the cradle, when my mother stopped her and asked to have the baby in her arms. She wanted to see what she had produced. She was overwhelmed with happiness to have a girl with red hair who looked at her. From that moment the bond between us was sealed and in a way we grew up together.

Mother was very handsome with her grey-blue eyes, a fine lined mouth and dark-blond hair. She was cheerful, had a great sense of humor, and was full of fun. She loved to be a mother and I wanted to be just like her. But at a young age I realized that this never could be.

We lived in a historic district called "Doorwerth", 4 to 5 miles west of Arnhem in the province of Gelderland in the Netherlands. This area north of the Rhine is very attractive with its hills only 30 to 40 ft. high, beautiful woodlands, small meadows, brooks, springs, ponds and winding roads.

We had two servants Jenneke and Cili. Both lived with us, Cili was from Westphalen in Germany but she spoke fluent Dutch.

The green-grocer, who came once a week, rode in on a horse and wagon. The other tradespeople like the baker, the milkman, and the butcher all came by bike. The baker had an enormous wicker basket on his steering wheel with a lid so that the bread was protected from rain and dirt. Every two days he would come from his bakery in the village Oosterbeek, heavily loaded, going up and down the hills for at least three quarters of an hour to bring us a wide assortment of fresh breads. When Hanneke and I knew he was coming, we would run down the path through the woods to a small fence-gate and ask him if he would give us a "krentebol" (currant bun); he always did.

A Golden Moment

We lived a very comfortable privileged life although I was not conscious of it at that time. My early childhood was more dreamlike. Everything was happy, always sunny and light. I stood one June morning under the trees in front of the long hedge of Rhododendrons. I must have been 4 or 5 years old. I was alone. I looked at the different colors of the flower clusters, one after the other, the pure white, the soft pink, the purple, the dark red, bush after bush. Bumble bees were going from flower to flower, hovering slowly above then digging in with great urgency. I felt the fresh cool air engulfing me. I sensed the smell of thousands of flowers. The stillness around me. The house in blazing sunlight. It was the overwhelming sensation of being at one with nature, revealing the secret of beauty of that fleeting moment. A golden moment.

When I was in the third grade at an elementary school in Oosterbeek, we had our first history lesson. The book started with the year one and on the first page was a picture of a man and a woman dressed in furs. What a revelation that two thousand years ago people were living and had to wear whatever was available in nature. To think of having no underwear on! How uncomfortable. I was glad not to be living at that time. Further I learned that in the year six Batavieren, a tribe, was living in the woods right where I lived. They built huts of tree branches. The roof had a hole in the center so that the smoke of the fire underneath could escape. It must have been pretty cold and drafty in the winter. I was so familiar with the woodlands, the brooks, streams and ponds, I could easily imagine their lives amid the hills.

Not far from our house was a path in the woods that led to a mysterious place on top of a hill. The path was about three feet wide flanked by tall Beeches and enclosed by dense woods. The grounds beneath the trees and beside the path were covered with a beautiful thick layer of green moss. It brought you to a wide open space with very large old trees. They stood there like pillars in a cathedral. The sunlight could not penetrate from above because of the thick heavy leaf canopy. The wind would rustle through the leaves or .... Were those voices of a long time ago? In the far corner we found a wall made of sand and moss, built in a circle about three feet high and fifteen feet in diameter. It was called the "Hunneschans"; "Hunne", the name of the people and "schans" meaning entrenchment. People would come here together to perform their rituals and speak justice. You could still detect the severity of this spot.

At the other end of the open space on the south side we could make an opening in the brushwood with our hands and have a peek at the view and see the river Rhine below us and across the river the meadows, the dike and many stretches of orchards and little farms. On a clear day we could see in the far distance Germany. During the war this historic spot was destroyed. People have restored it, but for me it will never be the same.

Doorwerth has a castle first mentioned in 1260, when Bernard van Dorenweerd was defeated by the Lord of Vianen. The castle might then have been just a wooden square tower. History tells us that it was an important manor, several times destroyed and rebuilt over the years. The castle was surrounded by beautiful trees. We had to cross a wooden drawbridge over the moat, then through a solid gate, coming into a courtyard with small buildings and stables and the castle itself. In the entrance hall stood a suit of armor of a knight welcoming us to a bygone age. Wandering through the rooms with the tall windows I could imagine myself sitting there with embroidery and looking over the meadows towards the Rhine. Downstairs was the scary place, the dungeons, with big nails hanging down from the ceiling. This ceiling could be lowered, so that the prisoner had to bend down or crawl, or finally not move at all. What a relief it was not to live in those primitive times.

A Favorite Garden Memory

When I was six or seven years old I woke up one day very early in the morning. The window was open and a soft breeze played with the curtain. The room was filled with the perfume of a Jasmine tree blooming opposite my bedroom window in the garden. So it must have been in the month of May that I was awakened by the song of hundreds of birds greeting the sun. Breathless and fascinated I listened intently to all the different gradation of all these sounds. Never did I hear such a unique beautiful concert. I was so captivated that I promised myself that from now on I would wake up early every day to hear this hallelujah chorus.

At that time there were very few cars. If one would pass our home, we would look up and see who and what it was. That did not happen very often. We never heard the din of airplanes but we heard the sounds of nature. They were significant because they were born out of silence. Even silence speaks. You become very much aware of what is around you and you become part of that. You feel connected. You are not alone.

Did you ever hear the song of a nightingale? What about the call of a cuckoo telling you it is going to rain? What about the calls of owls at night, the rustle of rodents on the ground, the buzz of bees and so many other insects? Did you ever hear the munching of oak-leaves by millions of caterpillars? "Yes," even that you can hear. Then I have to mention all the different noises the wind can make, especially when you are snug and safe in bed and hear the howling of a storm around the house. Violence exists in nature too. And a relief it is to hear the rustle of an oncoming soothing rain after a hot dry period.

There is always so much going on in nature that helps us to rejoice in our existence. One day I came home from school. It had been a difficult day and I was worried how I ever could be a good pupil. In a downcast mood I changed into my garden gear and went into the garden and started to clean out the leaves of the rose border. It was hard work, the wheel barrow was heavy with all the wet leaves to be dumped in the woods behind the house. It was cool and getting dark when I was finished. I came inside into the warmth of the kitchen and I realized that I was a completely different person. Gone was the worry, there was nothing I could not face, I was happy. From then on I knew that nature was my consolation, healing and hope as well.

We took countless walks with our Fox terriers "Whippy and Teddy". Every road and path in the area was known in detail. Mother taught us not to throw paper wrappings of sweets on the ground; never engrave your name in the bark of a tree; never hang or swing on a low branch of a tree, for it hurts the tree; don't destroy the mushrooms with your feet. For each mischief she had a wonderful Dutch proverb like:

Laat niet als dank voor aangenaam verpozen de schillen en de dozen.

Free translation: Do not leave the peelings and the boxes behind as thanks for a pleasurable time.

Another proverb: Gekken en dwazen schrijven hun namen op deuren en glazen.

Free translation: Crazy people and fools write their names on doors and glass windows.

We certainly were brought up to respect nature.

The War

The 10th of May, 1940, was a glorious spring day. Very early in the morning my mother woke me up and commanded me with a certain urgency to come to the balcony of the master bedroom. There stood my father in his bath-robe and pointing to many German planes flying over our heads. One plane came over the roof of our house so low that we could see the German sign under the wing. I had never seen a plane from so close by. It dawned on us that the Germans had invaded our country. We were at war. There was a big explosion and my father said, "That is the railway bridge from Arnhem to Nymegen over the Rhine, blown up by us to prevent the Germans an easy entrance." The explosion did not shock me as much as the fact that my father started crying. I had never seen him cry; I did not know that a man could cry. That was only for women and children. Most of that day was spent listening to the radio for more news. Mother was anxious for her brother Wim, who was an officer in the Army near Dordrecht. Was he fighting? What was happening to him? Of course we did not go to school.

In the evening we had our dinner and an orange for dessert. That was my last orange until I was seventeen years old. Eight o'clock was bedtime for Hanneke and me. We were not asleep when we heard the engine of a single plane circling around. Suddenly there was an intense whistling noise and the explosion of three bombs. Have you ever heard the explosion of a bomb just two miles from your home? Can you imagine what a terrible shock this was for us? I was curled up in bed, my heart beating in my throat, all muscles tensed up and listening for what would happen next. But nothing happened further, and now my reaction changed to rage: "What kind of person would do such a terrible thing? My father and mother are good people."

That was our first day of war. I want to point out to you that we children were brought up to respect other people, be polite, be honest, be obedient, and to keep learning to become a respected adult. It was never spelled out in so many words by my parents, but that was their wish for us and with love they would do whatever it would take to make that come true.

When a few days later Dutch civilians with small suitcases were passing our house, Mother recognized a couple. These people were fleeing from a fighting area called the "Grebbeberg." Dutch soldiers had their defense line there. I can still see in front of my eyes how Mother ran over the lawn to the fence to speak to them. She asked, "What is happening to you? What am I going to do when we have to move? Pim (my father) is too weak to walk, and then the girls...What am I going to do?" Mother was panic-stricken. I had never seen her like that. The couple comforted her and said: "Just stay where you are, maybe you do not need to move." Lucky for us that turned out to be so. I realized for the first time that my parents were just as vulnerable as Hanneke and I, and that was a revelation.

One night when everybody was asleep the front door bell rang. Mother heard it, put her housecoat on, and went downstairs to open the door. A German soldier stood in front of her raising his pistol to her chest and asking in a drunken voice where the nearest pub was. Father had awakened and wanted to know what was going on. He placed himself behind my mother. Slowly the pistol was lowered and Father gave him directions to the pub. Next day, recovered from the shock, Mother was furious and called the head of the civilian security saying that the German commander in charge should be informed of what happened to her. That was no way to treat civilians! I must say that when I read these lines, I was amused by her innocence about war. We still had a lot to learn. Civility between the enemy and us was already disappearing.

There were only five days of fighting in our country. After the bombing of Rotterdam the Netherlands capitulated. Rotterdam's inner city and harbor were completely destroyed. Our Queen Wilhelmina and her family had left for England. We were not pleased with that, but we understood later that this was the best thing she could do for our country. Since the outbreak of the war we dared to leave the house for the first time for a walk with the dogs. Approaching our school in the woods, we saw in the distance a troop of German soldiers around and in the building. Mother hesitated for a moment but then decided to move on, giving Hanneke and me instructions, "When we pass them, look straight forward, ignore them, do not talk to them. If they speak to you, you do not understand."

It was our first lesson in uncivilized behavior and very new to us. From then on we treated the "moffen," as we called them in this way. We hated them.

We received the bad news that Uncle William was seriously wounded. A bullet went through his arm and another one through his lungs. He fought for his life. In July, Mother took us to Dordrecht to visit him in the hospital. We were shocked to see him so white and helpless and he was in tears to see us. But he made it after many operations. On the way back home, we visited Aunt Miek (younger sister of Mother) at Rotterdam. Her street on the outskirts of the city had missed the bombs.

When Pearl Harbor was attacked by the Japanese, mother explained to me how and where this happened. It was terrible news she later went on saying: "Maybe this is a good thing for us. The Americans will wake up and see what is going on in the world, and maybe help us." Well you did and I cannot tell you enough how this filled us with tremendous hope that one day we would be free again. After all you were the good guys and would certainly win. For us, no matter what we had to sacrifice we were going to be loyal to our country and queen.

To give an idea what it is like to live under enemy occupation I want you to walk with me along a lonely road in the country. It is early spring. The sun is shining. There is a cool breeze but we feel the warmth of the sun penetrating our skin. It makes us feel good and fills us with energy and good cheer. In the distance we notice the clouds chasing each other. It is a warning that changes are on its way, but we are not concerned. Then a cloud appears before the sun and we feel for a short moment the chill. We keep on walking. The clouds are piling up and the sun disappears for good....not coming back for 5 years.

We lost our freedom. I always say that nobody knows really what freedom is until you have lost it. We speak a lot about freedom in the U.S. Definitely freedom does not mean that you can do what you like because you are not alone in the world.

Freedom is a conception limited by: Where we were born, the way we grew up and were educated and our understanding of religion.

Often we take our freedom for granted. We abuse or neglect freedom when we only think of ourselves. Freedom is based on morals that change with time. Freedom is bounded by rules, subject to a continuous dialogue. Losing your freedom means obeying the rules of the oppressor, the man with the gun, the powerful. You cannot talk freely anymore. You keep quiet in public places or you whisper. This was so instilled on me that after the war my mother had to say to me: "Stop whispering, you may talk now!"

Let me illustrate how careful you had to be with what you were saying during wartime.

From the archives of the town of Ede

Each town in the Netherlands had a civilian Protection Agency against air attacks, organized by the Dutch, just before the outbreak of the war. The following incident happened in the town of Ede not too far from where we lived. The head of the Agency, I call him Jacob, was sitting with his secretary, an 18 year old girl, in his office on Main Street. Looking out of the window he saw a German soldier passing by with a bad limp. Jacob exclaimed: "I wish every one of them walked like that!" Where upon the girl reacted:" Sir, you cannot say that, it is not right. You would not say that if he was an English man!" Jacob answered:" Yes, but I am a Good Dutchman!" The girl disagreed and wrote a complaining letter to the head of the town, the new burgomaster, who had been appointed by the Germans. Jacob was arrested and spent 8 months in a prison working camp.

Apart from losing your free speech we were also not allowed to listen to foreign channels on the radio. If the Germans found out, you would be sent to a concentration camp. The broadcast of the news from radio Orange in England was always at noontime when I was home from school. I had to stand guard by the window and when I saw a neighbor, a Dutch SSer (A collaborator with Germany) in black uniform passing by, I would warn my mother who was listening to the radio. Later in 1943 the Germans confiscated all radios to prevent people from listening. Newspapers were censored too. People working for Dutch newspaper companies found on their desk a form to sign, saying that from now on they could write and publish only the German version of the news. That meant that the Dutch population was not going to be informed of what really was happening in the world. German successes would be emphasized, defeats not mentioned. The papers would be filled with propaganda. If you were a loyal Dutch reporter, would you go along with that? Many refused and dealt with the consequences of persecution, having no job, no income, no safe name and home address. They had to go into hiding. People learned to read between the lines; to write and talk in codes.

On the radio we had a well-known program on cooking enjoyed by many house wives. Mrs. Lotgering Hildebrandt gave her recipes but many of them were information in code from the underground for the allies. Later she was betrayed, sent to a concentration camp and listed to die. She was liberated just in time at the end of the war. In 1947 we had a few cooking lessons from her at our school. She never spoke about her ordeal.

 Parents tried very hard to give us children a normal upbringing, as much as possible. Besides going to school (sometimes under hazardous circumstances,) we had our field hockey, tennis, dance and fine woodwork lessons. But the tensions and insecurity were always looming in the background.

 The winter 1940 - 1941 was a very difficult time for our family. After a long illness and bad heart condition my father died in March 1941. Soon after his death our beautiful house in Doorwerth was sold and we moved to a duplex house, two houses under one roof, just outside the center of Oosterbeek. Our new rented home was the last of nine houses on an attractive lane, branching off the main road Utrecht-Arnhem. In front of the house was a landscaped field, about a half kilometer in diameter. Our living room faced this field. Between the large beech trees we could see the main road with Hotel Hartenstein in the background. Hotel Hartenstein is now the Airborne Museum. During the Battle of Arnhem this was the headquarters of the First British Airborne Division.

Our home in Oosterbeek, Hartenstein laan, no.17 is on the left

Map of Hotel Hartenstein Area

I had to get used to a new school and also to prepare myself to go to high school, for which I had to do exams to be accepted. We saw now and then German troops marching down the main road singing loudly. The railway bridge over the Rhine was repaired and it was always guarded by German soldiers who had anti-aircraft there.

One morning in the summer of '43 our teacher took us swimming. We had a 15 to 20 min. walk to the river, where a section was made to a guarded area. Some kids got swimming lessons. I knew how to swim, so I was free. After an hour or so we had to get out of the water and get dressed. And while I was doing that suddenly there was a lot of noise of planes and near the bridge they started shooting. Quickly I finished dressing and got out of my cabin. There we saw how a plane was hit, broke in pieces, like a tree shedding its leaves, burning too and men jumping out. Some parachutes did not open, others were like tiny shining balls in the blue sky. We watched this with shock. Nothing we could do. It was too far away and the river in front of us. Besides the Germans would not have let us. We walked back to school, shaken and quiet. It was the first time we witnessed something like that.

I did my exam for the high school for girls and was accepted. This was in Arnhem. During the summer vacation the building was taken over by the Germans. It meant that from then on we had to share facilities with the high school for boys. My school hours were then from 1 pm till 5. My classroom was on the second floor. On the top of a flat roof across the street was an anti-aircraft gun. I always could easily detect that something was going to happen.

The soldiers would move around a lot and then the alarm would go off. Sitting on the last bench in the back of the room, it was my task to make sure that all the windows were closed and I was the last one to leave the classroom. We had to go downstairs and sit on the floor against the wall in the big hall. It was very scary waiting for what was going to happen. Lucky for us the alarms would go off again to tell us it was safe. Nothing had happened to us.

"In June, 1942, 460 important people, professionals, intellectuals, lawyers, professors, and ministers were taken hostage. If anyone took violent action against the Germans, some hostages would be shot.

Later all men between the ages of sixteen and sixty were in danger of being picked up by the Germans, to be sent to a work camp in Germany. Identification cards were issued to everybody above the age of 15. You had to carry it with you at all times. If you wanted to move to another town you needed a permit.

In the same year (1942) was the first raid on Jews, in Amsterdam. Most Dutch people were outraged about this, and many firms and companies like the railway system went on strike. The local rubber factory "Hevea" joined too. Of course the Germans reacted immediately, and everywhere bulletins were posted that everybody should go back to work, otherwise they would be punished. The ones who did not go back to work were picked up from their homes and questioned. The head of the factory was the interpreter for the interrogation and tried to help his men by asking the questions in such a way that they would give the right answer. He said, "You did NOT see the posted announcement, did you?" Some men understood and said, "No," but some were too honest and said they had seen it but disagreed with what the Germans were doing. So seven men were taken away in a truck and shot in the woods on the other side of Arnhem, all without a trial. One man was the father of two boys I played table tennis with.

I will never forget the English raids on Germany at night. It was a frightening experience and the raids were frequent. The alarms would go off. Then the searchlights started scanning the sky, and planes would be caught in the searchlight beams. I would hear the very distinct sound of the engines followed by the deafening explosions of the anti-aircraft shells. Mother would go tippy-toed downstairs all the time, listening to what was going on outside. We were scared. I stayed in bed thinking if I have to die, I'd rather be in my warm bed than downstairs, where it was cold since the stove was not lit. Sometimes it happened that a plane would be hit. It would get rid of its bombs and where would these bombs fall? One fell only a 5 minute walk away from us. Sometimes planes would crash. One fell in the woods near the home of my best friends. We snooped around it after the Germans had inspected it. Not a pleasant sight.

In September 1943 the Germans ordered us and all the neighbors on our street to leave the house in twenty-four hours and leave everything behind. Well, Mother was not going to leave everything behind. Somehow she got hold of a van and all the valuables, oriental rugs, furniture, silver antiques, and what have you were taken out of the house. Of course the Germans knew that this could happen and to prevent it a German soldier accompanied by a Dutch police officer, both on bikes, checked out the neighborhood. Fortunately the Dutch police officer was of the "good" kind and took the soldier on long tours to show him the countryside and so there was plenty of time for us to get things out.

For nine months, from Sept. 1943 to May 1944, we lived with friends on top of one of those hills along the Rhine in Doorwerth. The view from the house was perhaps the best and most beautiful of the Netherlands. Here we watched almost night after night the raids on Germany. It was forbidden to have any light shining out of the house. From behind the big windows we would look at searchlights scanning the sky. Sometimes indeed we would see the planes clearly. It was always a bit scary because of the terrible noise of the anti-aircraft. Everywhere you would see the sky lightning up and then after a while you could hear the rumble of bombs in the far distance followed by a tremendous red glow in the sky. I asked myself, how many people would be in that ordeal?

One day I was walking to the tram stop to go to the high school at Arnhem. The road was more like a wide path through the woods, first uphill and then its course was steep down. On top of the hill was a German watch-post manned by one soldier. It was the pinprick of my route. Very much like passing a scarecrow in a nightmare, but this one was alive. I was there alone; I felt his eyes fixed on me, maybe hoping I would look. Coming back it was even worse, because he could watch me from a distance climbing up. How I hated those spying eyes. He was not a human being, he was a soldier and our enemy.

I was now at the tram stop, waiting for the tram. I heard planes in the distance. It was sunny weather. The warning alarms went off, one at Nymegen, then at Arnhem, Oosterbeek, Deelen (airport) and the factory nearby. "What shall I do? Go home? Keep waiting? I don't think they will come here- it is all meant for Germany". I heard the rumble of bombs far away, I felt the vibration under my feet. Poor girl like me but living over there. What was she going through? Am I glad that I was born in Holland. All this is happening because of one crazy guy. Hitler. How was it possible that so many people believed this evil man? The "all clear" sounded, I waited longer and finally the tram came.

Looking back on this episode, it is astonishing that my mother let me go to school. We were so naïve, not realizing how dangerous it was to be outside when fighting in the air was going on. At any time things could happen without warning. Planes shot down. Anti-aircraft shrapnel hitting the ground. Bombs falling blocking the road. Despite all this, I went every day to school from 1pm to 5pm. I could catch the very last tram at 5.30pm going home. No more transportation after that and I was six miles away from home.

After nine months, the German-Wehrmacht vacated our house and the neighborhood. Mother furnished all the rooms as it was before. She said, "I am going to enjoy everything we have as long as I can." It was wonderful to be back in our own home. We discovered that the Germans had made a door opening in the wall between us and the neighbor. That turned out later to be very useful for us.

In June, after Mayday, we saw many German soldiers in wagons or on bikes or just walking, coming by on the main-road going towards Arnhem. It was obvious that they had left the fighting behind. They looked so stunned with hollow eyes that could not see anymore. Despite this shabby sight, a mean glimmer of satisfaction went through me. This was my enemy. War is war!

After the landing in Normandy (about four hours' drive from Arnhem), Montgomery came up with the plan to speed things up to the north by securing the bridges over the three big rivers, Waal, Maas, and Rhine.

The 101st U.S. Airborne Division was landed north of Eindhoven, the 82d U.S. Airborne Division at Nymegen, and the 1st British Airborne Division at Arnhem. It is the British Airborne landing that I experienced and will write about. You might have read the book, "A Bridge Too Far," by Cornelius Ryan, or you might have seen the film. With this writing I want you to know what a battle is like for an ordinary citizen, I was fifteen years old, old enough to understand what was going on. What you will read might be shocking and put you to tears. Don't be ashamed of that, for it shows your sympathy and compassion.

On Sunday morning the 17th of September, 1944, the alarms went off everywhere, Arnhem, Nymegen, Oosterbeek, and the airport Deelen. English fighter planes attacked all German anti-aircraft guns near bridges and the military airport Deelen. It was serious enough that the minister in church stopped in the middle of his sermon and let his congregation go home.

We had a late lunch and as we were about to leave the table we saw lots of planes appearing. Each plane was pulling a glider on a chain. The chains were dropped and slowly the planes disappeared behind the tree-line. We realized these planes were landing quite nearby, about three miles from our house. Our liberators were coming! We were so excited and overjoyed. Our town secretary, who lived behind us, passed by our house and told Mother to take care to have enough bread in the house. He was sure there would be some fighting. When that happens, go into the cellar and do not come out until it is over, he said.

An hour or so later German soldiers started to appear. They seemed nervous, running around, and not quite knowing what to do. I was watching from the living room, how they were getting ready for the fight, moving from behind one large tree to the next with their guns ready to shoot. I could hear the machine guns from the English getting nearer from the opposite side. I was standing next to the stove, away from the windows, looking for the first man to fall. It was shocking. It was horrible. I had never seen such action. I could not watch it any longer and ran to the cellar.

Mother had asked our neighbor, Mr. Rosman, if we could join them in their cellar. She wanted to be able to talk to a grown-up. The door between the two (duplex) houses became very handy. The cellar was only about 14 by 10 feet, maybe smaller. The ceiling was below ground level. It had a window opening with solid iron bars in front of it like a prison cell. That window was open, without glass.

We had settled ourselves in the cellar on kitchen chairs when we heard the ringing of our front door bell. There stood a German soldier, gun ready to shoot, saying that he was sure that there was a sniper in our attic.

He ordered Mother to lead the way up. So my mother went upstairs two flights to the attic, with the soldier right behind her back. It was lucky that there was no sniper, otherwise she would have been fired on from the front as well as from the back. The German soldier left, and Mother came safely back to the cellar.

We did not put any lights on, we just waited, listening to the shooting around us. We heard some shouting in German for help, but we did not move. Around 10PM it got very quiet; we dared to come out of the cellar. We thought the war was over for us, and we went upstairs to bed.

The next morning we were up at dawn. A cool mist was still on the field. We could see the shape of a few dead bodies here and there on the ground. Mother told us to pack our suitcases. Now I must tell you that a couple of months before all this was happening, we had heard from Radio Orange a warning. Anybody who lived near a river, near a big town, or near a main road should have a suitcase ready to move out quickly. I went upstairs immediately to pack my suitcase. When I came downstairs to show my mother what I had done, she started to laugh and said, "Oh, they will never come here!" Now we had to do it anyway. So each packed her own suitcase, a small one with room for a pajama, extra underwear, shirt and blouse, toiletries and jewel box. More would not fit. We put the suitcases in our own cellar on a shelf. Also a large box filled with all the silverware and a lovely antique clock from my grandfather.

We had breakfast and then went out into the street and walked to the main road to greet our freedom fighters, who passed by on jeeps. We had never seen a jeep. Some men walked and had marigolds in their button holes. We cheered them on and were fascinated by the spectacle. Our neighbor brought out his Dutch flag which had been hidden so long; we were not allowed to have our national flag or portraits of our royal family in the house.

Among the Airborne's was a known policeman from Oosterbeek, but now in a different uniform, who told us to go back home. "Put that flag away, we are not free yet. It is still very dangerous here. Further on the road they are fighting," he said. We obeyed and went home.

Later in the morning a large group of airborne were passing by near our house and had a rest on the side of the road. With a big bucket full of apples my mother went over to them and asked if they would like to have one. Of course that was the right thing to do. Then my mother asked for a favor. Could she have one cigarette? Packages were opened and she got a handful. Then she ran to our neighbor and said: "I won the bet." She had a bet with him as to who would be the first to have an English cigarette when we were free.

Hartenstein Laan showing No. 17 before the war

Hartenstein Laan showing No. 17 after the war

In the afternoon more and more English soldiers arrived and settled on the field, digging manholes all over, even in our yard and around the hotel. The whole area became headquarters. General Urquehart was in the hotel. Some Airborne's asked if they could have some water. "Sure, come in, use the kitchen and the bathroom, feel free." We admired their uniforms and all the badges. Suddenly the water started to taper off. We tried to fill the bathtub with the last bit, but it was not very much. That night we still went upstairs to bed. All the windows were intact.

Tuesday, the 19th of September, another pretty good sunny day. We got a whole group of Airborne's stationed in our house. It is exciting. A radioman has installed himself on Mother's bed. With earphones on he is getting and sending messages. One of the Airborne's, Alfred Waterhouse, and I sit on the terrace wall teaching each other English and Dutch from the telephone book. It is relatively quiet, shooting only now and then in the far distance. In the early afternoon lots of planes are coming over, dropping supplies on parachutes. Baskets with food and containers with munitions. The parachutes are in all colors. It looks like fairies in the sky. One container drops in our yard. I get a piece of the nylon material, it is bluish-green. In the evening we discover we have no more electricity. Mother places candles here and there so we can see where we are going. We want to go upstairs to bed. But the captain, Frank Ewens, tells Mother we should sleep downstairs. We get our mattresses and put them in the dining room on the floor. Again the captain tells us this is not good, too much glass. Then we put them against an inside wall in the hall. When we were ready to get under the blankets, the captain kneeled down and told us to try to get some sleep. He said, "You will hear a gun go off right in front of the house, but you don't have to worry about that. If something is happening we will help you to get to the cellar." What he did not tell us but what we later figured out was that he expected a big offensive from the Germans. Lucky for us it did not happen that night.

On Wednesday things started to change. I was getting something out of the kitchen when suddenly fighter planes dived out of the sky. I tried to run away to the cellar but Alfred put his arms around me and said, "You are safe, you are safe." I pushed him away and ran for the cellar. Then we got the first short spell of shell shooting. When it was quiet again we came out of the cellar. The large windows in the dining room were gone, and the house behind us had a big hole in the roof. I wondered how bad that was and if the people were all right. I walked outside. The Airborne in the manhole gave me a piece of chocolate. Boy, did that taste good. But then he quickly said, "Get inside" and I heard an explosion farther away. Coming inside the house in the living room, there was our group of Airborne's, looking ever so grave and troubled, Alfred leaning with his elbows on the tall radiator. There was no time for talk, because we heard the noise of an attack coming. When we started to run for the cellar I felt little things hitting my back and when I looked I saw a handful of candy scattered on the floor. I grabbed a few. Alfred had thrown them to me.

We were frightened, we were scared. You could hear in the distance the guns go off, followed by a high-pitched whistle noise and a nearby big explosion. If you did not hear the whistle, it was about to land on the house. There was another noise, like a kitchen chair scratching over the granite floor. When we heard that noise, you could feel your lungs squeeze as if they were going to explode. Very frightening.

Our Airborne group left. They let us know that they would be back the next day, but we never saw them again.

We hardly ever came out of the cellar any more. In the beginning when it was quiet for a while, we would go upstairs in turn to go to the bathroom. It was an incredible mess in there--of course, no water! Also the bathroom door was gone. One time when it was my turn, I was the last, the shooting started again. I was just halfway up the staircase, so I went back down. An Airborne noticed my predicament and took me to the toilet, neatly turning his back and waiting till I was finished. Through the high window (the glass was gone) I could see part of the top floor of the house behind us, and I thought I saw a German uniform! That was the very last time that I came out of the cellar during the battle. A bucket on the top stairs from then on was functioning as our toilet.

We had made ourselves comfortable with mattresses on the floor against the inside wall, and we had our pillows. Mother sat between Hanneke and me. Once in a while we would be visited by our English friends, taking a short rest. Cigarettes were passed around and once one was offered to me. I accepted it and Mother did not object! Did I feel grown up!

We did not eat much. We were not hungry. Sometimes our friends would come down with a can of hash of some sort and the pot would go around and everybody would have a mouthful or two from the same spoon. Mr. Rosman had picked some unripe apples from his apple tree before the ordeal started, and we each had one. In the beginning he had a bottle of water, but it lasted only one day. There was also wine in his cellar, and now and then we would have a taste of that. But surprisingly we were not thirsty. There must be something in nature that takes over and protects you.

One time after all hell had broken loose, a couple of guys came flying downstairs. One was a chaplain. He sat down on the bottom step, pulled his cap back and said in a cheery voice, "Well now, you are a bit on top of the war, aren't you?"

Mother, who spoke very good English, started to talk to him, saying how worried she was about the fact that we did not have an escape other than the stairs. If the house should catch fire and the entrance to the cellar be blocked, there would be no way out for us.

The iron bars in the window locked us in. It was indeed a dangerous situation, but nothing was done about it until Mother mentioned it again during a visit by a few guys. One of them found a file and removed two bars while heavy shooting was occurring. The man had to duck low now and then. It was a great relief for all of us when this was done.

Two houses on our street burned down. The noise was frightening. We heard people screaming "Come here, this way, this way!" We always would get an attack just at dawn or just before it got dark. Having the men visit us was welcome; somehow we felt a lot safer then. Many times we asked, "Can we get out of here to a safer place?" Always the answer was, "No, just stay here."

Sunday, September 24: The chaplain held a short service for the men in our house. Mother had asked if she could join, but it was too dangerous and they did not let her.

In the afternoon, a shell hit our home's cellar, just at the time that five men were busy putting a heavily wounded man on a stretcher in that very cellar. Now they needed another safe place, for all five were also wounded now. They were brought to the cellar we were in. The first one was in shock, repeatedly getting up and wanting to go upstairs. The last one was wounded in his chest, his head, and his foot. Our cellar was so small that the stretcher had to be turned around above our bent heads to position it next to me. The man was bleeding badly, the blood dripping on the floor. Suddenly the cellar seemed to be without fresh air. I was nauseated and was going to be sick. I kept repeating to myself,

"You are not going to be sick, you cannot make a mess, you will make it worse than it already is." So I got over it.

Next to the stretcher another man was laid down. He had a big leg wound and a stick-and-string tourniquet to stop the bleeding from his wound. He was confused sometimes and did not know where he was. I said some comforting words in Dutch, and maybe he understood. The space for the two wounded men was so small that each man's movement hurt the other, and then they would apologize to each other. One would whisper "Water, please water." But we had no water, so we gave him wine. After an hour or so they all were picked up and taken to a Red Cross post. They used my field hockey stick and made a flag of a white sheet with the red for the cross cut out from the Dutch flag and pinned with safety pins. Mother found it back in the house a year later.

    Monday September 25th was terrible. It changed our lives forever. The shooting went on and on. After a hit on our house we would hear the screaming of men running to escape. Nobody came downstairs to the cellar any more. In the evening Mother was called upstairs where the chaplain told her to write on the cellar door that we were civilians. That night all hell broke loose. The strip of sky I could see from my mattress was in flame. Even the dark cellar was lit up. It seemed that there was a hit somewhere on our house every five minutes. We kept our heads covered with pillows. One hit above our heads was so close that I prayed: "It was a short life, God, but it was OK. I commend myself into thy hands." Mother shook my hand: "Are you all right?" Yes and indeed yes I was all right. All fear had gone from me. I was at peace, nothing bad could happen to me. Everything seemed far removed from me, as if things were happening next door somehow. Later Mother told us that she prayed that if something had to happen to us, it should be her children and not her. Now that sounds very selfish, but it really was not. She wanted to take care of us, but if something happened to her, who was going to take care of her children?

    Slowly the fighting came to an end. We knew we had lost. When it started to get light, we heard German voices. We kept quiet. We still were not out of danger, for if the Germans thought we were English they might throw a grenade into the cellar. Finally they came down to the cellar, noisily eating but with their guns ready. We were ordered to stand up and each face in turn was lit up to make sure we were indeed civilians. After that we were allowed to leave the cellar. According to them the war was over. When I stepped out of the cellar I noticed just across the door opening a big pothole in the 1.5 or 2.0-inch thick granite floor. It was not quite through the entire thickness of the floor. The granite floor had saved us. I was too dazed to look any further. Mother went into our home, what was left of it. In the living room on the couch lay a badly wounded Englishman, his body wrapped in a curtain. Another man lay under the front door, which was leaning outward. A German soldier stood beside him, kicking his side with his foot. When the wounded man lifted his eyes, the German asked him questions, in German. This wounded soldier could not understand the question, so he closed his eyes again. Again the German kicked him.

Mother got the suitcases out of our own cellar, and the three of us started to walk. Our bikes in the garage were destroyed. Mother had her best winter suit on; it was made of an old suit of my father. I saw her drop one of her leather gloves. And, still in a daze, I thought, "What does it matter, one thing more or less?" I walked on, but then I came to my senses and walked back to pick up the glove. The field, the street, and the foot path were covered with bodies. I even had to step over one. My sister cried continually but did not know she was crying. And so we walked on, to the edge of the center of Oosterbeek, where the Red Cross was in restaurant "Schoonoord."

The English were taking care of their wounded. In the middle of the road was an English officer directing traffic. We walked up to him and Mother asked him what we should do. He told us to get away from the river and the main road and go at least five miles north, because of course we will be back. Then Mother saw an English doctor taking a breath of fresh air and asked him if he had something to calm Hanneke. His answer: "I am sorry, Madam, I have nothing, not even an aspirin."

Nearby people asked us to come inside. There was a water pump in a garden that was working, and we had a wonderful good drink. They gave us some food. Masses of German soldiers were also around. We asked one what we should do. His answer was, "You can stay here, the war is over!"

We decided to leave. It must have been around noon or perhaps a little after. We went up the road to the railway station heading north. We had gone a little way when we saw an old man in his best suit with a bowler hat sprawled dead in the middle of the road, his gold-rimmed glasses near his outspread hand. He looked as if he was on his way to a wedding, so beautifully dressed. At the same time there came an enormous German tank roaring down the slope. We knew it was not going to stop. We did not look backwards, it would have been too horrible to watch. We went on.

Over the railway bridge along the road there were many dead lying beside the road. At a few places the bodies were sorted out, English on one side, Germans on the other. There was nobody else alive apart from us on the road. Finally we got out of the worst fighting zone. We crossed the highway and headed to the national park called "Hoge Veluwe." We had gone there so many times on our bikes for a picnic.

There are a few houses on the beginning of the road and I asked Mother if we could ask for some water. I drank two glasses. We went further on the lonely road. We kept on walking until after sunset. The sky was beautiful and it was so still, as if nothing had happened. We had to hurry up now to get to the only house we knew was there. It was getting dark, and we had to consider the curfew as well. We got there, knocked on the door, and the people let us in. There were no beds, but they filled large burlap bags with straw to sleep on. For the first time in a week I undressed, had a wash, brushed my teeth, and put my pajama on. And then it happened. I started to shake all over. I had no control over my muscles. I was like an old shaky lady, not cold, not hot, and then I dropped off to sleep.

House in Oosterbeek

Exterior view of damage to No. 17

My bedroom

Otterlo

Otterlo is a small village to the north-west of Arnhem, about 10 miles distant. After the Battle of Arnhem in September 1944, my mother, sister and I headed from Oosterbeek for this village on the Veluwe.

It was crowded in the café "Hunter's Delight" in Otterlo. The door stood open and people were milling around inside. There were no seats to sit on and of course no drinks were served unless you would ask for a glass of water.

We had walked that morning from our first night's stay over at a lonely house on the road to Otterlo. Approaching the village we were greeted by Red Cross workers who gave us a loaf of bread. This gesture was well meant I suppose, but I could not help thinking "Why a loaf of bread here? We do not have a knife to cut it with! Something more to carry!" Where were we going? Where were we going to stay?

In the café someone offered mother help to bring her and the suitcases to the Red Cross in a local school, where she could secure an address to stay for the night. Hanneke and I waited for her while watching all the people around us talking in small groups. They were the locals of course, interested and anxious to know what was going on. There were lots of people from Arnhem who were forced by the Germans to evacuate. A minister from the Dutch Reformed church at Arnhem sat on top of a pool table listening to the stories and giving advice to the people around him

Mother returned with the good news that we had a place to stay in the attic above a bakery for the night. When the minister asked her what she was planning to do further, she told him that she would like to go to her brother in Amsterdam or to her sister in Rotterdam. But how to get there? No transportation no cars no trains! "Don't go to Amsterdam nor Rotterdam. There is no food. Your brother and sister have no way to care for you. They are in big trouble as it is. You must not do that" he pressed. But what to do then? Where to go?

Two students in their twenties were listening to this conversation. They had come out of their hiding places. [Remember that all boys and men between the ages of 16 and 60 could be picked up by the Germans for transportation to labor camps.] Many of my friends were also somewhere in hiding with false identification cards with false names. The students asked us many questions: What exactly happened to us? Was it possible for them to go to Oosterbeek? Could they find a way to cross the Rhine and join the Allied forces in the south? They wanted so much to help. Mother discouraged them. "There are too many Germans. You will be picked up in no time or even worse get shot. You are not familiar with the area. There is no water, no food and no electricity. I don't think you should do it."

Later that afternoon we went to the bakery, mother was warned that the owners were National Socialists (traitors). This meant we could not talk freely and we kept to ourselves. They gave us a meal. We had to climb a ladder to the attic where 3 mattresses with blankets were laid out on the wooden floor. The weather had turned cloudy, cool and windy, but here it was comfortable and warm with a nice smell. Of course we were exhausted even though we did not feel it, and soon were sound asleep, not so my mother. She did not like where she was. She felt locked up because she could not open the hatch in the floor. How could she get out if something happened outside? Also she worried about where to go next.

Next day we went back to "Hunters Delight." More talking about what to do. The students came back and after talking once more with my mother decided to go back to their hiding place. Then one made the suggestion: "Why don't you come along? We stay at a farm at Terschuur. We are with 40 of us in a big barn. The farmer and his wife are wonderful people. When we tell about you, I am sure they find you a place. There is enough food!" It sounded alluring and mother asked if this was a tenant farmer? "Yes" was the answer. "To whom does this farm belong?

"The landowners are Mr. and Mrs. C. They have a modernized farmhouse nearby. They are retired." The student said. "Is the wife's maiden name L.?" mother asked, "Yes" was the answer. "You bring us there; she is a relative of mine". She said.

We were lucky that we had now a destination. Terschuur is a hamlet and at least 12 miles from Otterlo. We managed to get transport with a Red Cross truck the next day and arrived at the farm on the estate "Groot Beylaer" on September 29 1944.

Terschuur

In the back of the Red Cross truck we had not been able to see much of the surroundings. The lorry was very similar to what the German military used in their transport of soldiers or raids on civilians. It had an open back with just a tailboard. It was covered from side to side with a dark canvas. There were benches inside so we were able to sit. The light was dim. All we could see was the sky above the tailboard and occasionally the tree tops flashing by. After less than an hour we stopped in front of an open tall iron gate.

Dick, the student, helped us by lifting us from the truck and we started to walk on a lane in a wooded area. Of course we were a bit anxious to see what was waiting for us, but the peaceful surroundings were soothing. We came to a farm in the woods and here the road took a sharp right turn and became a brick-paved street leading to a light spot in the distance. On our left were meadows laced with bushes, and on the right it was all woodland that shaded the road.

An old lady was walking about 400 yards ahead of us. She did not look back to see who was coming, instead she walked faster. Maybe she had a foreboding that something was in store for her. She disappeared in the light spot and a moment later we could see a white farmhouse between the trees. The front door was right beside the road and we rang the bell. A maid, dressed in black with a pretty white apron and a white lace cap opened the door. A gentleman came behind her, recognized mothers name and said: "Damn Toos, it is you! Come in. What has happened to you? This is terrible dear!" He led us to the living room where we met his wife, the same lady we had seen before.

Both were full of compassion. There was no hesitation in offering their hospitality. Immediately Jannie, the maid was instructed to get a bedroom upstairs ready for us. Yes, we could stay here. What a relief for us, especially for mother. We were so thankful for their kind-heartedness that we would do anything to make our stay pleasant for them.

Mr. C. adored England. He had been there many times before the war. His socks and shirts were always ordered from a store in London. He liked the English lifestyle and tried in many ways to copy it. Being very prosperous in his business, he had retired and bought this estate with 4 or 5 farms. The territory was off the beaten track. No main roads in the immediate area. To entice his wife to live in this isolated community, he had built her an eight-hole golf-course. The land was pleasantly varied. Parts were cultivated, small woodland sections, meadows and several streams crossed by rudimentary wooden bridges. There was plenty of wildlife. Before sunset you could see the rabbits playing around and the pheasants roosting in the lower branches of the trees. Of course it was illegal to have guns and shoot wildlife but the forest keeper kept us weekly supplied!

Mrs. C., who used to entertain hunting friends of her husband, was an excellent gourmet cook of wildlife. Even though there were two maid-servants in the household Mrs. C. did most of the cooking herself.

Four more evacuees had joined us, a middle-aged couple with an elderly sister and Arnold, a university trained engineer who we, Hanneke and I had to address with "Sir". He was 29 years old and we thought it was ridiculous that we had to do that. We would sit with nine people around a large mahogany table at mealtimes. Each one of us would have a small plate marked with our name and the weekly ration of 3 tablespoons of butter placed next to our dinner-plate. You could use it as you pleased, if you used too much you would run out before the end of the week that was all. On our walks we gathered all kinds of mushrooms. Mrs. C. was very knowledgeable about these and double checked every one of them.

When food was left over after the first round Mrs. C. would always offer us children a bit extra. All dishes and plates would go empty back to the kitchen. We had the bad habit of always talking about food while eating, even that we were so very lucky with what we had. Uncle Carl, the middle-aged gentleman composed a song:" What is for dinner tonight John (the butler)? And then came the answer, a whole list of delicacies in verse, imitating a well-known conductor. He did it so well, it was hilarious and we screamed with laughter.

Everybody had his or her chores to do. Hanneke and I would peel potatoes in the warm kitchen in the morning. We helped in raking leaves and getting the garden ready for winter. I learned to split wood with a big axe. When they heard that I could milk cows, I was asked to help farmer Blossem. I would go along a footpath, cross a stream then coming to a gate leading to a meadow where the cows were grazing.

One day when the sun was on its way down; it was very hazy however and I could look into the sun, I said a little prayer:" You can see me here all alone and at the same time you can see all our friends on the other side of the Channel. Give them warmth and make them strong so that we will be set free soon.

Shortly after we arrived at Terschuur Hanneke and I broke out with sores on our faces. Apart from the discomfort it was very unsightly. We visited an M.D., whose remedy was of no help. When mother received his large bill she was indignant that he had charged her while knowing that we were refugees. We then visited a homeopath who gave us the right herbal medication and soon our faces cleared up. Alas, now the men started to get boils on their arms and necks and they blamed us for it. We had brought this on.

Mr. C. decided that we all needed a bath. He had a windmill in his back yard. It was a modern one which made enough electricity to have lights at supper time and afterwards in the living room and kitchen for a few hours. We were very fortunate to have this luxury. All the farmers in our neighborhood used their old-fashioned oil lamps. Now having a real bath with warm water was like a fairytale come true.

The bathroom of our host was small and had a sit-bathtub. I had never seen that before. I filled the tub with nice warm water, sat in it and washed myself. As the top part of my body was exposed to the cold air I soon reversed my position- sitting in the deep part and with my legs on the seat but still under water. This was wonderful with my neck in the water soaking, relaxing and just waiting until the water cooled.

I don't know how long I stayed in that bath-tub, suddenly there was the voice of Mrs. C. saying:" Who is in the bathroom?" Now why are you still there?" She sounded impatient. Quickly I hurried out of the bath and dressed myself. I never forgot that wonderful bath because it took another year before I had a bath again.

Touched by the Secretiveness at Terschuur

Breakfast was served promptly at 8am. The nine of us would sit around the oval table. Mrs. C. sitting at one end would pour the "tea." We called it tea but it was more like colored hot water and it had a faint taste of some kind of blossom.

Arnold was late this morning. He had to come from a nearby farm where he had a bedroom. Most of the day he spent with us. He apologized to Mrs. C. and sat down at the table. Every night around ten, when everyone went to bed, Arnold would leave us and walked less than a kilometer to his digs.

It was November in 1944. The Germans had declared a curfew. Nobody was allowed to be outside after 6 pm. As we were in an isolated area in the country, Arnold ignored this restriction. Chances that he would be challenged were remote.

While we were eating our ration of two slices of bread Arnold announced: "Something very strange happened to me last night when I was walking from here. I always dodge from tree to tree on the side of the road because I don't want anyone to see me. I bumped into a man! I was terrified. It was pitch dark and I had to feel my way. I touched somebody. The man put his flashlight on, but not at my face and said calmly "Good evening," I responded "Good Evening." And resumed my walk home. I have no idea what he was doing there, he was Dutch, I can tell you that it was very scary."

Then Uncle Carl spoke: "Something very strange happened

to me last night. But before I go on I will tell you after breakfast when the girls (Hanneke and I), are out of the room." Well that was very disappointing for me not to hear more. But I heard it anyway later from my mother who, as always kept me informed.

Uncle Carl woke up in the middle of the night. He had his window and curtains open. The sky was so light and the ceiling in his room looked very red. That was not the sunrise! He got up and looked out of the window to see light beacons in the sky. One lonely man stood in the center of the meadow. He heard the engine of a plane circling above and slowly a parachute descended to the ground. It was obvious that the underground was at work receiving supplies of weapons from England. How exciting this was. Even here people were fighting for freedom.

New Shoes

Having just one pair of shoes, the pair we had on when we fled, and after all the walking we had done, it did not come as a surprise that they were worn out, kaput beyond repair. The winter of 1944 was approaching and something had to be done if we were not going to be housebound!

It is difficult to imagine now, what it was like not being able to go to a store and buy a new pair of shoes. There were none available anywhere. The only solution we had was to request the authorities for special coupons to buy wooden shoes which they granted us.

The nearest town was Barneveld, an hour's walk from where we were staying, had a wooden shoe factory. We had learned about Barneveld in our geography classes at school. This small town was known for its chicken and egg market, one kind of chicken was even named after the town "Barneveldse kip." Now there were no more chickens or eggs for sale. Food was very scarce.

Barneveld was also an historic place. Jan van Schaffelaar had jumped from the church tower in 1482. He was the leader of a group of twenty horsemen fighting against the Count of Kleef. He had occupied the village of Barneveld and settled in the church, where he and his men were beleaguered by civilians. Jan van Schaffelaar gave up and jumped from the tower whereupon he was beaten to death.

A memorial plaque near the church is still there. I looked forward to go and see it, besides it was a nice break from the routine of daily chores.

We left for Barneveld on a cold damp day, walking through the woods for two-thirds of the way on private land and then along a country road leading to the town. We found the factory and Hanneke and I got our first wooden shoes. They were yellow-orange colored with a simple design on top. Don't think you can walk straight away on wooden shoes! It takes some time to get used to. We certainly could not walk back with them on. After we got home and had some practice the wooden shoes with the leather slippers inside became quite comfortable.

A month after the war, in June 1945, I gave away my wooden shoes, one with a hole in the bottom, to two Canadian soldiers who were pleased with their Dutch souvenirs.

November 1944

The weather was getting colder and daylight became shorter. The cows were brought into the barn. Only a few yearlings remained in the field, they looked forlorn when I passed on my way to the farm. It was warm inside the barn. The condensation, caused by the body heat of the animals, was dripping down the small windows and the concrete walls. A row of cows faced each other from both sides of the barn. In the center was a platform from where the cows were fed hay, sugar beets or turnips.

Farmer Blossem had twelve cows of which nine had to be milked. He had room for more, but the authorities of the German occupation did not allow this. Farmers were, like everybody else under strict regulations. All the produce had to be accounted for. Each bucket of milk was measured and a large part of the harvest turned in. Collaborators, Dutch Nazi volunteers in green uniforms would control this by holding surprise inspections. Lucky that farmer Blossem had a watch dog on a chain near the house. As soon as a person entered the property the dog would bark violently. I never arrived without being noticed. People in hiding, and there were many, sometimes in the chicken coop where you could not stand straight up, would be warned of the possibility of danger. The family would be on the alert and make sure that everything was properly in order.

Usually farmer Blossem was waiting for me to arrive with a one-legged milking stool and a clean bucket in his hands. He would fasten the hind legs of "Irene", a placid cow. She was named after our second princess of Orange, the younger sister of Queen Beatrix.

When I was ten years old I had been taught by the brother of Nelly, a servant, how to milk a cow. Now I had fun practicing it every day. With my wooden shoes on I would make a giant step over the trench, sit down on the stool under Irene and worked her teats. Like most cows she would first resist, tightening her muscles, but then she would relax and a good stream of milk would splash in the empty bucket. In ten minutes, or so it was all done. Farmer Blossom would check on me and see if I had milked Irene to the last drop. After helping with feeding the cows I walked back home.

The best part of the day, was coming into the living room where the stove was burning. Nine people gathered there waiting for the light to disappear. There was no use of electricity until dinner in the dining room. Hanneke and I would sit on the floor knitting a sweater from the wool that was given to us. There were not enough chairs for us all. It was so peaceful to see the rabbits in the fading light playing under the trees and to hear the cackle of pheasants finding a roosting place in the lower tree branches. Slowly the darkness would take over and with it our quiet voices coming to a stop. Everybody united in his or her own thoughts, thankful that another day had safely passed by.

Another Terschuur Story

Identification cards were issued to everyone over fifteen years old in the first or second year of the war. I got mine in June 1944 and lost it in September during the Battle of Arnhem. A few months later I lied about it when we were interrogated by a couple of Germans and one Dutch collaborator. I told them that I was born in 1930 instead of 1929 because I did not want to give a lot of explanation! What was that interrogation all about?

One night, the nine of us were sitting around the stove in the sitting room as usual playing our favorite game; writing down all the place-names we knew beginning with a certain letter. That particular night was pretty cold with a full moon. We heard the noises of some planes but we tried to ignore them. We heard it so often! Then one plane's engine began to sputter. Mr. C. looked up from his paper and said with his eyes on the ceiling: "You don't drop your poopy on me". Not a minute later Jannie, the maid rushed into the living room: "Sir, there are two parachutists coming down, you can see them clearly". We all wanted to rush outside but then we remembered the curfew and the danger of being shot at. So we stayed inside.

A farm nearby had forty people hiding in a barn, although you would never know it, for when we passed this farm it always looked deserted. Many of these people in hiding must have been very much involved with underground work (Dutch resistance). We later heard that they were quick to rescue the two parachutists before another farmer, who was a traitor, came to the field. He found a parachute and took it with him to his farm. He thought the material was beautiful for his wife to use. (At that time we did not know what nylon was.) He waited two days before he went to the German authorities to tell them. This was lucky for the rescue operation, giving extra time for the parachutists to get away.

When the Germans finally came in a truck to investigate, they came too late! Everybody was prepared. We were all ordered to come out of the house and stand in one line. The Germans took the watches of the men to look for foreign inscriptions and they checked each identification card. It was obvious that we were not involved and they departed, but not before stealing a box of candles that Mrs. C. had just taken out of storage.

Bad News

One day, in the last two weeks of Nov. 1944 at Terschuur, I was on my way to the kitchen when my mother stopped me and said in an anxious voice: "Mr. C. wants to speak to me, I have to go to their bedroom." (This was the only place where one could have a private talk.) I wondered what this could mean as I waited for her near the door. After a short while Mother came out of the room in tears and said with a broken voice: "We cannot stay here any longer, we have to go." She ran upstairs; she wanted to be alone.

It was devastating news. No explanation of why we had to leave was given. It filled me with indignation. How could they do this to us? How could they do this to my poor mother who had gone through so much already? It was not fair. After all we had arrived in this place before the other refugees. I was absolutely certain that Hanneke and I had not given any trouble or bad behavior. Where would we go? Who would take us? I was worried. We never found out the reason for why we had to go,. At the dinner table that evening Mrs. C. asked if we would like a second helping as she usually did, but I answered with a stiff, "No thank you." "Oh how come, you never say no?" she went on. At that moment I felt the pumping of my blood through my neck veins. I wanted to cry out loud but nothing came. There was an uncomfortable quietness loaded with tension around the table. But it passed because I kept my mouth shut. Later Arnold found us an address at Ede, bless his heart.

Ede

It was snowing when we left Terschuur before 6 am., walking in the dark to Arnolds digs where somebody with a horse and wagon would come to bring us part of the way to Ede. But nobody came and so we walked back to the house. Except for the maids everybody was still asleep. Mother did not like to face the family again and made the decision to walk the whole way to Ede. That is fifteen miles. We never had made such a long walk. The falling snow had turned into rain. Hanneke and I were wearing wooden shoes that made walking on ice difficult. With each step forward you slid a bit backwards. Because of the foul weather nobody was on the road. There were no cars, trucks or buses. Most cars were confiscated by the Germans and there was no gasoline anyway. It was lonely on that rural road, but we were lucky that we were healthy and had been fed well at Terschuur, so we could endure our fate. We knew where we were going. It had been difficult to find a place, for most families had already their extra rooms occupied by refugees. It was almost dark when we arrived. A middle-aged couple whose children had left home welcomed us. Mrs. Leton led us to our room upstairs. We were exhausted. We had been on our feet for twelve hours with very little rest. No wonder that Hanneke and I sat down on the first possible seating which was the double bed. "Not on my beautiful bedspread!" cried Mrs. Leton. We jumped off and promptly the bedspread was replaced by an ordinary cover. And that was the beginning of our stay at Ede.

The three of us slept in the double bed. It was a bit narrow but it was nice and warm. We lived without heat and there was no electricity. Out of respect for the privacy of our host and hostess we spent most of the day in this room; after all, we were dependent on their goodwill and would not like to give cause for any bad feelings toward us. It was already difficult for them to feed us with what supplies they had.

For breakfast I would have two slices of a grayish bread topped with a teaspoon of tomato paste. That was pretty good! One might have to stand in line for hours in front of a bakery to buy one loaf of bread. It was mostly women, girls and old men who would do the shopping. It was not unusual to see a person faint from weakness or hunger. Often you came home empty-handed. The ration coupons were worthless because the supplies were not there. The only way to get food was to go to farms and beg for it. When you had no bike, you would walk. People used little carts or baby carriages for transportation of the goods. Money had no value. You traded with silver-ware or linen or whatever was valuable. It was difficult for us, we had nothing to trade.

Mother wanted to help Mrs. Leton so she borrowed her bike. It was a bike with wooden tires which made it very uncomfortable to ride. On a cold misty day she was on the road for miles, visiting the farms in the area. Towards the end of the day she was successful. A farmer's wife gave her a canvas bag filled with potatoes. On her way home she was stopped by a German soldier. He asked her what she had in the bag and then took it from her. He wanted the bike as well, but Mother pleaded so hard that he let her go with the bike.

From then on Mother knew she had to find another way for us to survive.

Ede II

At Christmas 1944, after we had been in Ede for a few weeks, Mia Leton, the twenty-one year old daughter, came home and like most students she could not go on with her studies. There was no food. The whole country was in disarray.

Mia took me immediately under her wing. She volunteered for the Red Cross and took me along. We had to walk twenty minutes through the town to get to a school where the Red Cross had made its residence.

Ede was a garrison town. All the barracks were occupied by German soldiers. Mia and I prepared ourselves well to not meet the enemy face to face, if we could help it. We had our heads covered with shawls, walked fast and avoided eyes. Luckily we were never stopped.

The Red Cross post was used as a shelter for travelers on foot or bike. Most people were on tour from the West hunting for food. But there were also men who had escaped the German work camps in the nearby battle zone. Sometimes small groups of men with a leader would arrive. Nurse Terlingen, the visiting RN of the town, who had taken charge of the Red Cross, would only speak to the leader. She asked us not to talk to the group of men. I suspect that these mysterious groups were in the resistance, maybe escaped English soldiers, who were in constant danger of being detected. It was better for us not to know. Everyone could stay for one or two nights. The floor in an empty classroom was covered with straw where people slept. I had to promise nurse Terlingen to never go into that room.

I suppose this was for hygienic reasons. Some people were sick and had dysentery.

Food was distributed in the late afternoon. It came in a "melkbus", a very large tin container special for milk used by farmers. It consisted of a watery, whitish soup with undefinable lumps and it smelled horribly sour. A head count was held and then we estimated if there was enough for everyone. If not, we just added water.

Years later people asked me if I was hungry at that time. I have to say that I was not hungry enough to eat that stuff ...I could not. Clearly, I was not starving!

My task at the Red Cross was to clean the floor in the corridor with water, there was no soap. I also had to do some odd jobs for nurse Terlingen who was often like the other helpers on the road visiting patients, I would stay behind, just so that someone was in attendance. Usually the building was empty in the daytime.

One day all the nurses had left with their bikes to go to farms and beg for food. Nurse Terlingen gave me the keys to the cupboard where the bread was stored. She told me to take good care of the keys, but I left them in the cupboard door and then started to clean the floors. While I was busy, I heard the rattling of the keys. Alarmed I rushed to the office where I found a man in his forties with his hands behind his back. I knew straight away that he had taken the bread. Standing in front of him I commanded: "Put that back where you found it!" He did. No further words were spoken and I kept everything that had happened to myself.

One day a sixteen-year old boy arrived. He looked more like a twelve-year old and was much smaller than I. He came from Rotterdam where German soldiers, in a raid, had taken him to work for them in the battle zone. Piet was too skinny and could hardly handle a spade to dig. The German soldiers had no use for him and let him go. Nurse Terlingen took pity on him and allowed him to stay for a while. Piet adjusted quickly to the course of things. He helped whenever he could. He was like a little brother. Late one morning he came into the office and said to me "I have a surprise for you, we are going to eat." Out of a bag he carried, came four potatoes he had stolen from the German soldiers.

Now, I had seen in the town the passing of a horse-drawn wagon with a German soldier sitting on the driving box, with the reins and a whip in his hands. The wagon was open at the back and filled with a layer of potatoes, bouncing about with the motion of the wagon. Lots of children were running behind the wagon stealing potatoes. The soldier, angry and frustrated turned in his seat and used his whip to chase them away to no avail. It was a hilarious sight but it never occurred to me that I could have joined those kids. But Piet had done it.

We decided that we were going to have fried potatoes. We had no fat or oil of any sort but Piet got hold of some candle ends. He melted the candles in a small frying pan on top of an open empty can. In a hole underneath the can he made a fire of little bits of collected woodchips. This miniature stove worked wonders. We had the most delicious fried potatoes in wax ever consumed and I have never forgotten it.

Ede III

Helping the Red Cross was a godsend for more than one reason. It was nice to be away from the house where we stayed. Although we all did our best to keep control of ourselves and the situation we were in, there was always an undercurrent of uneasiness between the families. We knew that there was not enough food. How long could we last? We heard the rumor that the allies were progressing, but that was not around us. When would we be liberated? That was the important question.

At the Red Cross I was confronted with other people's problems. Often they were a lot worse than ours. We were definitely not alone in this misery. As a matter of fact we were pretty well off. We had a roof above our heads and people cared. At the Red Cross I was treated as an adult. What a relief not to be just a schoolgirl. How wonderful to take part in that adult world. A transformation had taken place. Like a snake I was shedding my old skin and getting ready for the next stage of life. What could I do to help?

A plan took shape in my mind. What if I could go back to Terschuur to stay with farmer Blossem and his family for a week? This was the family I had helped with feeding cattle and milking cows while being in Terschuur. It would mean one mouth less to feed while I was away. Maybe I would be lucky and farmer Blossem would give me food to bring back with me. It was going to be a long trip, fifteen miles. We had done it before. This time I would be alone, but that did not worry me. I was heading through isolated farmland that was so much safer than at Ede which was full of German soldiers. I knew that I could do this walk alone.

Mother was not particularly enthusiastic about my idea. "Do you really want to do this?" She asked and added: "Well I have to think about it, I will tell you tomorrow." The next day, without much talk, Mother gave her permission. Only I had to promise that I would come back exactly after one week, leaving on Saturday and returning the following Saturday.

So I set off with a resolute mind, carrying a small bundle with my pajamas and toiletries. There is not much I can remember of that walk to Terschuur. It must have been very uneventful. The family Blossem was astonished to see me back alone. They took me in as a lost daughter. Aagje, the eighteen year-old daughter made room for me in her bed in the garret. We had to climb a ladder to get up there. It was very dark and musty. There was no window. A lighted candle barely showed a table and her bed. I had never slept with a stranger in one bed, but I was too tired to care and I slept well.

The food was basic but plentiful, potatoes and cabbage or other winter vegetables and on occasion some meat or bacon in the hodgepodge. After the meal farmer Blossem would read out of the Bible and prayers were said. The ritual was new to me and I was fascinated by their devotion. Only now do I realize what a fortunate girl I was to live for a week with that farmer's family in such an intimate way.

When Friday arrived I asked, embarrassed, if I could have some food to take home. For days I had been worried how to ask for more food when these people already had been so generous to me. But on the morning that I left, a bag made of cloth filled with 5 lbs. of flour was given to me and then I went happily on my way home. The sun was shining with some clouds here and there in the sky, perfect weather for walking. I enjoyed the changing landscape of woodlands and small meadows with brooks in between on private grounds. After half an hour I came to the road to Barneveld when I heard the familiar sound of Spitfires. It always was exciting to find them in the sky and follow their course. There were three speedy planes flying in formation, the sunlight making them shiny like silver against the blue sky. I stood still, enjoying it, seeing them come back and then going around in a wide circle. What were they up to? Then I saw them diving down to earth with tremendous speed, so fast that even my stomach was somewhere in my brain. The high-pitched noise was deafening, followed by the rattling of artillery, then the explosions and then the revving of the engines to get back up and up in the sky. They circled around, again getting set for the next dive down to the same target. It happened three times! What dare-devils! It was too close for comfort, a mistake might be made or bullets could go astray. So I jumped into a manhole on the side of the road to take cover. The whole event lasted less than ten minutes and then I moved on.

When I came close to the town, I saw black smoke billowing above the trees, it was where the railway tracks were close to the road, and a freight train must have been hit. How fortunate that I had not left earlier from farmer Blossem's.

I got home without any other trouble. My courageous mother was very happy and thankful to see me safely back. We had been a whole week without any communication.

Leaving Ede

When Mother heard the news that a good friend of ours had moved to the province of Groningen in the North-East of the Netherlands, she contemplated going there as well, if possible. The constant worry about food was just too much to bear. Poe, our friend, stayed with his cousin and her family on a big farm in the Oostwolder polder. There was plenty of food and the place was far removed from warfare. What was keeping us from trying to get there too, to that land of milk and honey? We were well aware that it was going to be a tricky undertaking. Oostwold was about eighty miles or so from Ede. Impossible to walk that far under the circumstances. We needed transportation. But there was none. Furthermore, we needed a pass from the German army to cross the river Ysel. This was the border between East and West in the Netherlands and under strict control by the German Authorities to prevent illegal activities and to stop the flow of masses of people hunting for food in the East.

In order to receive that pass, Mother had to go to Apeldoorn, a trip of about twenty miles. The bike with wooden wheels was borrowed once more and it took her a good part of the day to get to Apeldoorn, where she arrived just five minutes before the German office closed at 3 pm.

This visit was not like going to the post office for a stamp. No she was going into the den of a lion, completely depending on what kind of treatment she would get. Was this German officer civilized? Was he in a good mood? Would he listen or would all her efforts be for nothing in one stroke? Mother was lucky. Maybe because she was the last customer that day. Maybe because of her good looks or the way she presented herself. The officer gave her a pass valid for only a few days.

At the Red Cross, Mother investigated the possibilities for transportation. Nurse Terlingen was very helpful. Once in a while a Red Cross truck was allowed to go north to collect potatoes. She arranged for us to take a ride in this empty truck.

We had to come to the Red Cross before six pm. the day before we were going. This was because of the curfew. Nobody was allowed to be on the street after six pm. The truck would leave at four am. We waited, huddled in blankets, for it was cold at night, there was no heating in the building. But no truck came and the next morning we went back to our residence. A few days passed by when we heard that the truck was going. Again we prepared ourselves for the move as before. This time the truck came. It had a driver's cabin and an open wagon edged off with wooden boards. Behind the cabin was a tall contraption blowing smoke out of a tall pipe. This was the device that made the truck run. It was a stove. We sat on the platform against the wooden board at the back and now and then got a whiff of smoke in our faces. The driver asked us to look out for planes and warn him immediately by banging on the little rear window of the cabin. From his place he could not see or hear what was happening in the sky. The Allies were attacking any moving vehicles on the road. These were their instructions and we knew it. If it happened, the driver would stop and try to get us off the truck and then we would take cover. It was still dark when we left, a beautiful clear sky with a half moon. Covered in blankets we did not mind the cold, and the soot on our faces did not harm us either. We were lucky to have this ride and best of all there were no planes. Arriving at the bridge at Deventer, Mother had some anxious moments Hanneke and I did not know about. Mother had falsified the pass, for it had already expired. Instead of the expiration date of the sixth of March, she had written a one before the six changing it to "16". The German guards who did the checking did not notice and with just a little waiting we passed through without difficulty.

The truck went as far as Gastelernyveen, a hamlet we never had heard of, and left us at an inn where we had something to eat and drink. From there we started our walk to the town of Wilderfank another 9 or 10 miles or so. It was cool but sunny weather. There was already a touch of spring in the air. The landscape was new to us. We walked with happy anticipation, mother in the center, each carrying her suitcase, changing it from one hand to the other to give one arm a rest. So we walked mile after mile on an empty road, except for one horse and wagon that passed us. The man looked at us with great curiosity but did not greet us and kept to himself. I thought: "Can we ride with you?" But I let the opportunity pass by. We still had our pride! The landscape changed. There were no more trees and bushes. The land was open and we could see Wilderfank in front of us in the distance. The town appeared not to be attractive, one canal along one road along one row of houses, all in a line that reached to the horizon. There was no end to it.

Mother carried a letter from an acquaintance whose mother lived at Wilderfank. The mail delivery was not reliable in those days. So the lady was very happy that mother took it upon herself to deliver the letter. She made sure in her writing that her family would help us if we needed it. We looked for the address and stopped a man on the street to ask. He pointed to the horizon and said: "Do you see those trees in the far distance? Well it will be just a little further. You will be almost in Veendam."

We suddenly felt very tired. This was a long, long way to go. The disappointment was hard to take but we kept going without much fuss. Finally we passed the trees and found the address. We were exhausted. Mother's hands were bleeding. We could hardly talk. Mother rang the bell. The door was opened. Mother stretched her hand out with the letter and gave it to the lady of the house. She took it but did not look at the letter. She just opened the door wide and invited us in, her face shocked by the sight of us and full of mercy. What a blessing to have people on earth with wide open arms.

After waiting in the hall way for a while, a bedroom was prepared for us. That was all we desperately needed – sleep and rest. We could not talk. A couple of hours later we were woken up. Dinner was prepared. The large family, all adults, had gathered around the dining-room table. My seat was low and squeezed between two people.

One lady smiled at me with sympathy and invited me to sit down but words were not spoken. I felt very drowsy. I could only see the two faces opposite me. Everybody was intently listening to the conversation going on between Mother and one of the sons. We had a fantastic meal. In front of me was a large dish full of steaming hot crumbly potatoes, something I had not seen in a long time. I heard Mother say, "I want to go to Oostwold." Whereupon the man she spoke to got up from the table and said: "I am going to work for you right now!" and left. We went back to bed, our stomachs filled and feeling safe.

The next morning we heard of an ingenious travel arrangement made for us. To get to Oostwold one had to travel from Veendam at least another twenty kilometers. Now it happened that there was a wedding that day in a hamlet halfway in the direction we had to go. Of course no carriages were available in that tiny place. One had to be rented from Veendam and the other from Winschoten, a town up north. What a coincidence that our host knew about this wedding, so he could arrange for us to travel in the empty coach to the wedding place, wait out of sight until the wedding was over, and then continue the journey in the other empty coach to the north.

The ride was long and monotonous, but we were so thankful that we did not have to walk. The family we had left gave us a loaf of sweet black rye bread to eat on the way. Mother gave me two slices. It was delicious.

The coachman was quite willing to bring us to Winschoten, but when he heard that we wanted to go to Oostwald, he was not so happy. It meant for him another sixteen kilometers on the road. Finally, he grudgingly agreed.

We arrived in the late afternoon at our destination. The farm was just outside the village on the road to Delfzyl. It must have been quite a sight for this farmer's family seeing a coach appearing and stopping in front. The whole family came out side including Poe. We were welcomed and made to feel at home. It had been a long - long trip all the way from Ede.

War Events on the Farm in the Oostwolder polder '1' March 1945

Living on a farm was new to us. I enjoyed the experience and learned a lot. A polder is a tract of low land reclaimed from a lake or sea and is surrounded by a dike. The farm had a stately façade and looked like an important townhouse. The annex was a huge barn twice the size of the house where the grain was collected. The living area and bedrooms were on the ground floor. The basement was partly above ground and had windows. There was a second floor that had one bedroom with a high window cut out of the sloping roof. This used to be the bedroom of the two daughters who had left home; now it was mine.

Shortly after we arrived Mother, Hanneke and I were separated from each other. I stayed at the farm. Hanneke went to the next-door neighbors who had a daughter of her age. Mother went to another farm one and a half miles away. This was decided before we could talk about it and we accepted it without much thought. It meant we were separated for the first time since the battle of Arnhem. It did not bother me, but later I have wondered what it did to Hanneke. Mother spent most of the daytime with us. We were lucky that when war activities started again, we were together, thank God. Our hostess, Aunt Ena as we called her, was a middle-aged widow. With the help of her two sons, sixteen and nineteen years old, and a foreman she ran the farm; this was not an easy task for her. The boys kept very much to themselves. They lived an isolated life and had no social activities. Everybody spoke the local dialect, which was difficult for us to understand. We were looked upon as strangers and not real Dutch people like them; they told us so. Despite their stand-offish attitude, they were at heart kind people. It was just a matter of "Getting to know you."

Soon after our arrival a pig had to be slaughtered. Hanneke and I were not allowed to see this happening. Days were spent in the kitchen to cook the meat and pack it in sterile glass jars. I learned how to make butter.

On Monday mornings, the wash had to be done before eight o'clock breakfast. Everybody helped. Clothes were washed in an enormous kettle of soapy water over a wood fire in an open shed outdoors. My job was to stir the wash with a big stick. With the help of a washboard and wringer, all the wash was done by hand, then hung on lines to dry in the ever blowing wind.

We had no idea what was going on elsewhere in our country. But one day Poe called us to come in the parlor, a front room looking over the fields. He pointed out six German soldiers building a shed two miles away on the small road to Midwolda across the fields. We had not seen any soldiers since we crossed the bridge in Deventer. So we were surprised and could not figure out what they were doing there. With binoculars we followed their doings day by day; here was a nice diversion from the routine. After ten days or so we saw them throwing liquid out of buckets over the shed, which then burst into flames. Each soldier had a bike fleeing to Midwolda. What was happening? Poe told me to go upstairs and look out of my bedroom window to find out if I could see the Dutch flag in the church tower at Winschoten. I climbed on a chair and saw with binoculars the flag flying in the wind eight miles away. I screamed from happiness and everybody joined me. Winschoten was liberated.

But when would we be liberated? Days followed. We were in a mood of eager anticipation. Finally the day arrived when we heard the sound of many motor vehicles in the village. We could not see them. Then allied soldiers appeared crawling on their stomach to the road outside the village and, seeing there was no danger of being shot at, they got up and walked back to the village. A moment later two jeeps with allied soldiers passed our farm. We were the second farm in the row of four on that section of the road. How disappointed we were to see them coming back to settle at the first farm, less than a quarter mile away from us. We were left in no man's land. We knew from our previous war experiences not to go outside. We had to wait for them to come to us and they did. It was a Polish regiment. Their English was almost incomprehensible but that did not matter. We were happy getting to know them. Aunt Ena gave them bacon, received enthusiastically, and their short visits were repeated.

Still, we were in no man's land. In the North, near Delfzyl, there was a pocket of German soldiers who could detect with hearing devices the noise of passing jeeps on our road. They started shooting. At first I could not believe I saw a projectile hitting the side of the road without explosion. I thought I was imagining it. But the next shell was near the farm; we rushed downstairs to the basement. Then another shell hit one of the bedrooms upstairs. All the glass windows in the basement shattered. One splinter grazed the skin of Mother's cheek. It was not serious but she was shocked. She told me later that she had the feeling that the war was hunting her down. The whole episode lasted less than ten minutes. Immediately I realized that the basement was not safe for us and I was worried. I should ask the Polish soldier what we should do. I saw his jeep in the driveway and ran around the house to find him. He recognized me and greeted me with a big smile and I urgently asked him: "Is it safe to be here"? Somehow he understood what I was saying (I could not speak English). He casually waved with his hand and said: "Oh, you will be all right." Then I looked straight into his eyes and asked again: "Are we safe here? Tell me the truth."

The tone of his voice changed and much more softly he said: "No, it is not safe here". I ran to Mother and asked her: "Shouldn't we move to a safer place, going to where it is liberated?" A meeting with the neighbors was held and we all decided to move out together next morning. We carefully planned how to do it, what to take with us and where to go. Three families were involved, total of sixteen people, seven adults, six teenagers and three small children. Two large wagons pulled by horses were loaded up with mattresses, linens, blankets, pillows, pots and pans and all the food available. Everything was well organized. I was lifted up on top of the pile and sat by myself very high. I felt like a general surveying the landscape. The soldiers in the village let us through on the way to Winschoten. The road was clear of rubble and there were no signs of force of arms. It was peaceful. The sun was shining. I enjoyed the ride.

Winschoten

We were welcomed at Winschoten by hundreds of Dutch flags red white and blue decorating the buildings. The streets were crowded with smiling people. There was a mood of exhilaration lifting the burden of the past. We were now on liberated ground and we were safe.

We stopped in front of a tall townhouse that stood empty. It belonged to the parents of a member of our group. She found her parents living in the attic. Previously, the Germans had confiscated their home. We were welcome to stay there.

The front room on the ground floor had a large table with fourteen chairs. It seemed to be arranged just for us. The back room became our common bedroom. Here we laid out all the mattresses. Each family had a section of the room except Mother who had an upstairs room all to herself. She had an infected tooth and was not feeling very well. A local dentist helped her and after a week she recovered.

Cleaning teeth was a problem for everyone. There was no toothpaste. The brushes were made of bare wood with boar hairs. Every time you brushed, you would finish with loose prickly hairs sticking in your mouth. Months later I received my first plastic tooth brush from George, a Canadian officer. I was very happy with that gift.

Sleeping together in one room was quite an experience for all of us. There was no electricity. We made sure to get ready for bed before full darkness. Each person respected the privacy of the others. I slept safe and sound. The men left before dawn and then was it time for the rest of us to get up.

In the morning, just as we were wondering what to do, we heard in the distance a band playing. Canadian and Scottish troops marched with fanfare along the streets to the square to have the reveille. Immediately we followed fascinated by the music, the bagpipes and the colorful uniforms. Youth from everywhere were joining too. We got very excited. Spontaneous we participated in the ceremony, mimicking the soldiers, standing at attention while the anthems were played, saluting the flags when raised. Late in the afternoon the ceremony was repeated with the taps and again we were eager to play our part in it. These ceremonies took place every day while we were at Winschoten and I will always remember them as a dignified celebration of our freedom.-

The war had come to an end for us. Mother and I vowed: THAT WAR SHOULD NEVER HAPPEN AGAIN.

For nine months we had lived day to day to survive, never questioning our future.

Oosterbeek Monument – 50 years later

It was late April 1945 when we were back in the polder again. The fields were freshly plowed and lay open to receive the seed. A sign of a new beginning. I was watching the clouds chasing each other in the strong wind high above with the sun making fleeting shadows over the landscape. The spell captivated me and for the first time I asked myself, "What are you going to do?" I answered, "I will go back to school, work hard, become independent, and help Mother."

With this new beginning my war stories have come to an end.

Afterword

It is more than seventy years ago that all this happened. Millions of people gave their life. 72,000 Dutch civilians starved to death in the hunger-winter 1944-1945.

It is my mission to let you know what war is like. I do this for all those people whose screams you never heard, whose lives were changed forever.

What causes war? Are we really interested in a peaceful world, or have we given up on that idea?

War is the worst thing we do to one another.

Wars prove how pitiful we are, not being able to hold on to peace.

Wars have been with us since the beginning of time. Civilizations have disappeared. Is our civilization also going to disappear?

We cannot make the world better by ourselves. We need each other, we depend on each other no matter how far we live apart. We have to learn global thinking.

I learned that love and compassion make our lives worth living.

We don't live for ourselves alone, but we also live for others and because of others.

Always realize that many sacrifices have been made so that you could continue to live.

Don't take life for granted.